To Casada
Stay Blessed
Pay it forward

3/2015

Scarred,
BUT NOT BROKEN

My personal experience as a single mom; deployed to Iraq In Support of Operation Iraqi Freedom 2003 to 2005

Yolanda Jones
Disabled Veteran

authorHOUSE®

AuthorHouse™
1663 Liberty Drive
Bloomington, IN 47403
www.authorhouse.com
Phone: 1-800-839-8640

© 2011 Yolanda Jones. All rights reserved.

No part of this book may be reproduced, stored in a retrieval system, or transmitted by any means without the written permission of the author.

First published by AuthorHouse   4/28/2011

ISBN: 978-1-4567-6154-7 (e)
ISBN: 978-1-4567-6155-4 (dj)
ISBN: 978-1-4567-6156-1 (sc)

Library of Congress Control Number: 2011905778

Printed in the United States of America

Any people depicted in stock imagery provided by Thinkstock are models, and such images are being used for illustrative purposes only. Certain stock imagery © Thinkstock.

This book is printed on acid-free paper.

Because of the dynamic nature of the Internet, any web addresses or links contained in this book may have changed since publication and may no longer be valid. The views expressed in this work are solely those of the author and do not necessarily reflect the views of the publisher, and the publisher hereby disclaims any responsibility for them.

This book is dedicated to all single mothers; women of domestic violence; people whom have been discriminated upon and those who struggled to have a voice. I pray that this book provides you the courage and empowerment to have hope, to take a stand, to advocate for what is true and what is right.

Special thanks to God, for he allowed me to experience all that I did; so that I would be the voice and catalyst for change and to my mother, who never wavered but has been my greatest support. Mom, I Love You!

PREFACE

Spending a year in numerous locations in Iraq was an experience that will forever be remembered. Consequently, having been cross-leveled into an Engineering Unit; whose mission was to rebuild, which was destroyed by Sudam and his followers that, of itself, was very frightening. For starters, I was cross-leveled to a former MOS, 92A20. My initial job description involved, dispatching vehicles, ordering vehicles parts, driving to and from class IX warehouses to pick up ordered parts; as well as, conducted PLL inventory and supervised a junior supply soldier. Additionally, my duties required supervising other junior enlisted soldiers when ordered. Although, these job descriptions didn't seem as though I would be in harm's way; thus, it was the opposite.

However, I was a soldier of one who sought to help others with regards to illegal matters, involving racism, domestic violence and sexual assaults that were undergoing within this Engineering Unit. It later became a price that I eventually had to pay; by being intentionally placed on dangerous convoys, ostracized, ridiculed, berated and taunted; as a repercussion measure, to keep quiet and to "mind my business." Nevertheless, by the Grace of God, our convoys always were spared and missed coming into contact with road side IED, by a slither of a hair. Hence, that was only a minot portion of my punishment; to keep quiet and that was the beginning of the fear of not knowing if I was going to become a casualty.

Thus, during my time at Camp Striker-Camp Victory-Bagdad, we experienced incoming rockets, mortars and planted IED; near the defac, everyday; sometimes, every other day. Later, when we packed up and relocated to Fob Duke, it wasn't so bad. Then, toward the end of our mission, we returned to Taji which, was also known as Camp Cook. Here, is where I experienced more life and death situations. We were under constant attacks from mortars and incoming rockets 24/7. I recalled many instances, where I left certain areas and soon after that, the same area was hit. For example, I was given a half day to report to work; which meant, I was not to report to work until after lunch. Well, as I headed out walking down the road towards the job site …not long for it was but less than five minutes, when I heard a loud noise, behind me. The noise was loud enough and the impact was hard enough to knock me from my feet. I turned around and I noticed smoke coming from the sleep quarters; the same areas where I had recently just left; maybe had walked a good 250meters, if that. At this point, I wasn't certain what was the damaged, or even if anyone was injured. Immediately, I ran back to my tent, to see if there were any casualties; however, no one was in the tents. Thus, the smoke had come from the shrapnel that had landed on another tent. We also noticed the rocket had left a large hole in the cement wall that sat twenty-five paces behind our sleep tents.

My Experience and My Story of Living Eternity of Hell on Earth............................

CHAPTER 1

The Attack on the World Trade Center-Twin Towers (9/11/2001)

It was a regular day at work; I had just walked out of my office to inquire of the receptionist my next consumer for intake. It was a little after 8:46am at which, the receptionist informed me that a plane had just crashed into the North Tower of the World Trade Center. "What?" Yes, the place where I once visited, as a little girl growing up in Brooklyn, New York. I could not believe my ears. I thought the receptionist had misreported the news, until I had seen it with my own eyes. [She had a hand held black and white TV, it was showing the recaps of the first plane flying into the World Trade Center-Tower]. All of a sudden, I saw the second plane hit the second Tower. At that moment, I thought I was watching a movie. My mouth dropped. My heart began racing. I could not believe what I had just witnessed. Although, I could not stop thinking about my relatives, whom may had been either working or tending to business in those buildings.

The World Trade Center was known to be very busy towers which various establishments took occupancy. I wasn't certain who, but I knew I had a relative employed at the Twin Towers. Immediately I telephoned my family in Texas to inquire whether they received any news from any relatives, working that day. At that time, my mother was also shaken and was not certain if my older sister or my brother-n-law or one of my cousins or uncles were working in the Towers. However, all we knew at that moment was that a family member(s) were employed there. The hours of uncertainty were pain staken; to say the least. And, because I was unable to remain focus at work, I became very emotional which resulted in me having to leave for home early. When I arrived home, I continued to phone my relatives in Brooklyn, Queens, Bronx, Manhattan and New Jersey, although, due to the high volume of calls coming into New York, I was not able to get through to any relatives, at that time.

Naturally, the phone lines were overcrowded, and this went on for hours. Finally, I received a call from my mother for she informed me that I had an uncle who had recently been laid off, the day prior. It resulted in him not being at the site, the following morning. Although the news was a relief, neither I, nor my families were able to be totally relieved; since, we still had not heard from my older sister and my brother-n-law, as well as, other relatives that were not accounted for. The feeling was indescribable, to say the least. The not knowing. The waiting. I had mixed emotions. I didn't know if I was waiting to hear the news or the death of a loved-one, or if I was waiting to hear news that a relative was located and had been airborne to the hospital. Either way, I was preparing myself psychologically for the worst; although, I was already there emotionally.

The night was long. I can't recall getting a wink of sleep. I believe it was a day or two later that I received confirmation from my mother that all relatives were accounted for; both maternal and paternal relatives. But, although our families were safe, we all still mourned. We still lost many of our own (New Yorkers). How could something so devastating, hateful, ruthless and insensitive happen, so close to home; in our backyard? Hence, many people lost loved-ones, yet the irony to this attack was that many races, ethnic groups, socio-economic status and professionals came together.

My Uncle, the late Sheikh Ismail Abdur Rahim was one of the many, who provided onsite counseling. Many Leaders, such as the Christians-Jewish-Catholics-Muslim; as well as other Leaders came together to "set the prayers for the dead"; for the first seven days. My uncle selflessly officiated prayer vigils with Governor Pataki, in attendance. My cousin, who is the son of my late uncle, he too; along with his reserve unit partook in providing assistance. My cousin and his Reserve Unit pulled guard duty for three months, on site and in the morgue area. In addition, they transported supplies and equipment to and from the site (ground zero). My cousin shared briefly of his experience, in that, people from hundreds and thousands of miles away, even from other states, provided their assistance.

According to my cousin, he never seen anything like this before, he reported that "People were all standing and lined up on West Side Highway[which leads up to the World Trade Center] handing us bottles of water and thanking us for just being present."

9/11 will always be a day of remembrance.

CHAPTER 2

The Possibility of Deployment; what does a Single Mom to Do?

After the events of 9/11, although I continued to report to work, things still were not the same. Neither, was I able to remain focus. There always remained a possibility of being deployed to Iraq; in support of Operation Iraqi Freedom. Although, nothing was definite. Years later, another event had occurred. The attack on the 507th Ordnance Maintenance Company; who by report had taken a wrong turn in the city of Nassiriya; which, had resulted in the death and injury of many of their soldiers. Although I had been a reservist at this point for ten years, I honestly believed that if I hadn't been called to support Desert Storm or the War in Somalia then, my chances of being called in support of Operation Iraqi Freedom was going to be slim to none.

However, I later received information from my First Sergeant and Unit Commander that due to the recent ambush on the 507th, there was a possibility that our Unit would be called to active-status. At this point, I did not wait for our unit to be called; instead, I immediately began making plans to move my children back to Texas to live with their maternal grandparents, just in case I was called to active duty. At least, my children would not be stuck in North Carolina waiting on family to arrive to get them. Hence, I also knew that it would take awhile to complete all legal matters, re: the Power of Attorney and locating the appropriate schools; as well as building the rapport and briefing with the school principals and teachers.

Therefore, I submitted my resignation at my place of employment of three years. Then, I transferred my reserve unit to a unit in Grand Prairie, Texas. As a single parent, I had mixed emotions... ......I was honored to be part of history, but at the same time, I was afraid of what to expect; especially, to step off the plane, into enemy territory. I began to question the unknown. Were we going to be attacked? Ambushed? Was our plane going to be hit by an RPG / Mortar? Were our vehicles going to roll over onto an IED (Improvised Explosive Device)? Are we going to be held captive; like the unit before us? If so, will I survive to return to my children? Will I end up a paraplegic; resulting, in having to live with my parents because I can't take care of myself and my children? What if I die; will my ex-husband try to come and collect on my behalf and try to regain custody of my children? I say "my" children, because I was always mother and father to my children. Everything they obtained and/or learned, they acquired from me and/or their maternal family. Thus, I began to self-sabotage myself through my negative thoughts; although my thoughts were negative, could they have also been real? An inner discernment of what is to happen? I continued to think......my brain was on over-load. If it were a socket, it would have blown because of the high current/voltage.

Now, here I was as a single parent making this transition, for myself as well as for my children. My thoughts were, even though I had a Power of Attorney drawn to relinquish my parent's full access to provide care for my children. Could at any time their father try to fight my parent's in court to gain custody to force my children to relocate to Chicago to live with him and his dysfunctional family? The thought now became my biggest worry and fear. No longer was getting killed in Iraq my fear or even being held hostage. No. Huh.... that was minot, compared to the thought of my son returning to Chicago with his father and being subjected to the street life of hanging out in strip clubs, getting involved in the maladaptive lifestyle of drug trafficking, gangs, gambling, making illegitimate babies and the possibility of prison. As for my daughter, I vision her being in the wrong place at the wrong time; resulting in getting raped or involved in drugs, prostitution and becoming a teen mom. I was now looking at a much bigger picture of reality. What does a single mom to do?

CHAPTER 3

Transferring of Units; in Preparation for Deployment

During my transfer from one Reserve Unit to the Next, I was transferred from a Quartermaster Unit in Kinston, North Carolina, to 223rd Maintenance Unit in Grand Prairie, Texas. When I arrived to this Unit, I was informed that the Unit had been placed on high alert and had a possibility of being deployed to Iraq in support of Operation Iraqi Freedom. Therefore, monthly reserve weekends were tailored around maintenance of the vehicles, but for some reason, some male soldiers had other agendas. It was apparent that many of the male soldiers were always making sexual advances at the female soldiers. Each drill weekends were worse than the last. I felt like a piece of meat that was being thrown to the slaughter. This Unit had a male capacity of at least 90%; the other 10% appeared to be female soldiers. It became very difficult to report to drill because although there were few, the majority of the male soldier's behaviors were inappropriate. And, if they were approachable, you would have to be a female who were either batting your eyes or switching your behind; just to get the male soldiers attention. I, for one, wasn't buying into it and neither was I going to tolerate such behavior. I began to think, there is no way I can see myself going to war with these soldiers who seem to have only one thing on their minds; sex and lust. The sad part of it all were that many of these soldiers, whether male or female were married; yes, and were behaving like this. It makes one ask, why get married, when you can't control the beast within?

I remained with this Unit for about one month; until I requested to be transferred to another Unit; that was adjacent from this Unit (across the parking lot). It was the 16th LSO (JAG-Legal Support Operation). Since, I held a Bachelor's Degree in Criminal Justice, I was immediately accepted without any hesitation or reservation. Because of the recent incident with the 507th, it appeared that all Reserve Units were on high alert; including this Unit. Again, I had no problem with fulfilling my military obligation. At least, I was now with a Unit who would be most knowledgeable in my rights as a single mom and the fear of my ex-husband trying to regain custody of my children, in my absence. I now was very relieved, for the necessary documents had been generated and made official. I no longer felt overwhelmed or worried about my children; I was now ready to deploy. During my attachment with the 16th LSO, I held various hats. My primary job description was a Training NCO. Although, there were many times I was utilized to assist in other capacity; such as, generating Power of Attorneys and updating Life Insurance Policies, for many soldiers assigned to various Reserve Units on the installation. Death once again hit home.

During my few months attached to this Unit, a few of our own were killed while in their helicopter or traveling in a Chinook. Once again, my mouth dropped and my heart sanked for their family here at state side. I remember this tour was a voluntary mission for one of the soldiers, in particular who had recently bought a home in Hawaii and I believed was about to retire; upon their return. Therefore, I became sick to my stomach. To think, I have always used as a cliché, "tomorrow is not promised."
Yet, the start of this war had made that evident and a true revelation and confirmation. Thus, I was still waiting to deploy, but no orders...

CHAPTER 4

No Deployment - ETS - Reclassified - Re-enlisted - Deployment Orders

I had now relocated and transferred from North Carolina, to get my children settled with their maternal grandparents. Then as a result, I enrolled them in school and collaborated with their principles, which were in preparation of being deployed. Although, my transitioning and arrival in Texas was 3/2003, it was now fall and I had not received any deployment orders. My ETS was slowly approaching, which was 10/2003. I went back and forth in my mind, not knowing if I wanted to re-enlist or not. At the same time, I wanted to be part of something bigger than myself; I wanted to make a difference. I wanted my family to be proud of me. More importantly, I wanted more than anything not to become a single mom statistic. I wanted my children to be proud of their mom. In spite of the struggles, that we endured, without any emotional or continuous financial support from their father.

I wanted more than anything to be someone that my children could see as a mentor. Not, the celebrities or the athletes, whom, tend to falter because they're human and too often are placed in high regards, as though they're without fault......but many do. As a result, society and parents are becoming upset and being judgmental. No, we can't get upset with the celebrities and the athletes when our children want to mirror them. They're not our child(ren) parent(s) , WE ARE! Parents need to begin accepting RESPONSIBILITY and ACCOUNTABILITY for their behaviors and how they raise or do not raise their children; and, stop BLAMING everyone else for their LACK of parenting........Then we can look in the mirror and say, I have raised a responsible young man or young woman to be a responsible man or woman in society to do the right thing.

Well, as I thought about it hard and long, I decided that I enjoyed putting on this uniform. The feeling was unexplainable....I just knew that I wanted to remain in this uniform and to serve my Country. I enjoyed the camaraderie. I enjoyed the structure of the military. I enjoyed it so much that I could type an error on a memorandum that I wasn't worried about getting fired------of course, I wasn't allowed to use white out, but I knew all I had to do was to re-type the document. It was no big deal. I also enjoyed that I had a voice; as long if the transmission was tactful and/or requested to speak freely, I could say what I wanted and not be reprimanded. Although I knew as long as I remained in the military, I would always have to fight off sexual advances; however, I knew I could hold my own. Well, I decided to remained in the military, provided that I could be reclassified as a 27-D (Paralegal).

I was beginning to really enjoy the legal tasks assigned to me. Therefore, I re-enlisted and successfully completed my first phase of my Paralegal requirement, which was an online course. I had a secured date to begin Phase II of my Paralegal requirement which was to attend 27-D school in Nebraska, on 1/2/2004.

However, all came to a halt, when I received my deployment orders on 11/22/2003. The date of my deployment orders was on my son's 18th birthday. How could I go home and wish my son "Happy Birthday" and out of the same breathe, say, "Oh, by the way, I just received my deployment orders to Iraq, today." This was supposed to have been a special day for him; yet, I've turned it into a birthday that would eventually scar him. I tried to request to get my orders amended, to attend his high school graduation which would had been 5/2004; however, my request was denied.

CHAPTER 5

Cross leveled; A-Co. 980th Engineering Battalion Operation

I received my orders to report to an engineering reserve unit, located in Dallas, the following month. Their need was for a 92A-20 (Sergeant / Automatic Logistic Specialist). As I reported to this unit, I had no idea which platoon I was assigned to, neither was the already established soldiers or Unit Administrator helpful. Instead, I was instructed to line up for formation and thereafter, I would be placed with the correct platoon. So I did. After formation I was identified and introduced to my correct platoon. My platoon sergeant was an arrogant-egotistical-womanizer, who thought he was God's gift to women. So, he thought. Yes, he was a SFC (Sergeant First Class), who's blemishes had for so long gone untouched and swept under the rug. He believed that he was entitled. He only associated himself with those of his own statue or higher and disconnected himself from his squad, both emotionally and physically. He was very obsessed with himself-very grandiose..... Did I mentioned, he was arrogant and a womanizer? Yes, he preyed on the weak, as well as, abused his power/title/position in more ways than one. Hmm, does Narcissistic ring a bell?

Hold that thought. There's more of this, later in the book.

While cross leveled to this Unit, I was basically detached from my previous Unit. Now I belonged to A-Co. 980th Eng Battalion. Things with this unit appeared to be going smooth, so I thought. However, I was assigned to the Motor Pool. It appeared as though I was the only female assigned to this section, until later in the month, other soldiers from local Units and abroad were also cross leveled. One thing I noticed with this unit straight off the back was that there were no boundaries... Soldiers did whatever they wanted to do. At the start of my task, I would oversee and initiate driver's licenses to the soldiers who were authorized. Although I made several attempts to set boundaries, by instructing soldiers to report to the Motor Pool at a certain time, there were always a selective few, who tried my patience.

There was one male soldier in particular. He was a PFC. For some reason, this particular soldier thought, he too, was God gift to women because of his cute dimples and his swave demeanor. Thus, I had to turn this soldier away more than twice, due to he continuously wanted to challenge my authority; although he eventually received his government driver's license, during the instructed time. This soldier was assigned to be the Commander's personal driver, while in theatre (Country; Iraq). And, although every soldier had a "Battle Buddy"; so did I. However, this particular soldier became my additional support and one of my angels, during my entire deployment. Later in this book, I will share how I assisted this soldier in directing him to speak with legal, re: a racial incident. Since, receiving my deployment orders on November 22, 2003 I had to report to this crossleveled unit daily, in preparation for deployment, it was similar to an 8-4 or 9-5 job.

At the end of the day, I came home and spent as much time as possible with my children, because I knew at any given time I was to leave. And, I did not know when. Every second and every minute was valuable to me. For when the time came and when I would have to depart I did not know if seeing my children was going to be my last. So, as I spent as much time with my children, I began to think about how people; in general, tend to take the precious of life for granted. Such as, putting off calling a love-one until tomorrow; or not completing a project until next week or putting off from going to visit a friend or a loved one until next month.

All the not knowing, if the roof is going to collapse; if an 18-wheeler is going to high-plane into your lane; if a driver runs the red light and side-swap your vehicle and sending you into a tail spin; or if a plane looses fuel and altitude and drops from the sky; or if the gas pump ignites while you're fueling your vehicle; or if some faulty electrical wiring in your home causes a fire while you and your family are asleep. All of these incidents have actually happened; at some time or another. Who's to say that these events cannot happen to you or to a loved-one, whom you've put off seeing until tomorrow?

CHAPTER 6

Boarding the Bus to Fort Hood; My Best Friend's Pain

Well, the time had arrived, and it was time to board the bus to Fort Hood. Although I saw from watching the news and observing families saying their good-byes that I knew these families were feeling some since of pain, which were evident by their tears. However, I never saw the tears fall from the faces of the soldiers, boarding to leave for deployment. Was it because they didn't want to be a disgrace to the uniform, by crying? I always was curious about the soldiers level of pain missing their families; being away and out of reach from their loved-ones. How did they cope? How were they so able to hold back their tears? I was curious, no longer.

I felt my own pain; it was as though my heart was being stripped from my chest. I witnessed my eighteen year old son loose the ground from under him. He was not able to stand which resulted in my uncle and stepfather having to hold him up, each standing beside him. I had never seen my son cry, like he did. My son was one who had a bubbly personality, always the life of a party and the clown of the class. The teachers all through grade school and into high school adored him. My son had always been my best friend. Some would say, your children can not be your best friend.....well, I beg the differ. My son knew that I was his mother. There was never any doubt about it. Hence, my son respected me and he has always come to me for advice. I have always set boundaries with my children; whereby, leaving no room for misinterpretation or confusion.

Too often I have heard the older generations say, "children are supposed to be seen and not heard." Well, what I have to say in response to that would not be appropriate for this book......maybe in my next. Consequently, my children and I've been through some very hard times and all we had were each other, without any help from their father. As a result, my son took on the roll of the "man of the house", by making sure that no-one hurt me or his younger sister. He was always helpful around the home, by repairing things that were broken or would offer to help prepare the meals.

At age seven, I began teaching my son how to wash dishes; sort and wash his own clothes. He was taught how to prepare breakfast, such as, flavored pancakes, french toast, scramble eggs, grits and oatmeal. My son's first dinner meal was Hamburger Helper. [Laughing]. You couldn't tell him anything. [Laughing]. After awhile, we ate just about every different style of hamburger helper on the grocery store shelf until, I felt as though I was turning into a hamburger. [Laughing]. Anyways, speaking of oatmeal, my children grew up on old fashion oatmeal.

There were many nights when my son was five and my daughter was one and a half years old, and all we had in the pantry was old fashion oatmeal, a loaf of bread, and a gallon of milk which was all they ate before going to bed.

Sometimes, I would mix up a batter of flour and milk to fry some bread in a pan to make some bread, when I ran out of our loaf of bread or eggs to bake corn bread. I had to improvise.

I remember walking to a phone booth in the winter to call my older sister to ask her to wire me $25. At that time, I was living in Illinois and had recently transitioned into my new place from a domestic violence shelter. However, I had no gas for my car. Basically, I was trying to start over. I was a fulltime student and enrolled in a local Junior College. My son was in grade school and my daughter was in daycare. You would have thought that I had a history of a drug addiction the way my sister gave me the third degree, just by how she interrogated me for asking her to wire me $25. She wanted to know, "What's wrong? Why are you asking me for $25? What do you need $25 for?" Yes, even though I explained to my sister that half of the money was going towards gas and the other half was going towards groceries. The end of the conversation went like this................."Well, let me discuss it with my husband and I'll get back with you................ [Smirk] I told my sister, you know; don't even bother. That was the last time I've asked my sister for anything........................That was over 20-years ago.

I've always been told growing up that if you don't have anything else to eat, always have some old fashion oat meal, a loaf of bread, a bag of flour and some can milk and you'll be surprised what you can do with it. But, most importantly, you'll never go hungry. And you know, my children and I never did. I even remember when we didn't have a toaster, I toasted my children bread on the heater, which what we called up north the radiator. [Laugh]. I laugh now, to keep from crying because we truly were just getting by. Furthermore, I had too much pride and was too embarrassed to call my mother and family to ask for help; let alone, tell them how hard we were struggling. I, on the other hand, would eat a slice of bread and a glass of water, because I didn't want to eat all the bread from my children, and Lord knows, I did not like oatmeal. So, many nights eating oatmeal was what my children ate, before bedtime. Until one day, a neighbor and a good friend informed me about state assistance, which I later applied for and was approved. No shame. Anyway, I digressed a little, but I'm sure you're still following along.................

Let's just say, seeing my son collapse and lose ground was a sight that I don't ever wish on my worst enemy whether married or single. But, I signed on the dotted line. It was my choice to re-enlist. No one placed a gun to my head. Neither was I under any duress. I had a sound mind, when I re-enlisted. I knew what I was doing.

Anyway, as I sat on the bus, I noticed that my daughter and my mother were smiling and waving. I told myself that something was wrong with this picture, because the men (my son-uncle-stepfather) were wearing sad faces and my mother and fourteen year old daughter with braces were waving and smiling. I had always been told that I was born into a family of strong Black Women. However, never in a million years would I have believed it, had I not witnessed it, that my mother and daughter would be waving, instead, of crying.

CHAPTER 7

The Beginning of the Secret; Keeping the Secret at Fort Hood

I remember standing by my wall-locker for it was in the evening hours. I had just finished taking a shower. All of a sudden, the birth of the secret. She had just entered the barracks and it appeared that she was crying which was evidence by the sound of the sniffing coming from across the barracks. No other soldiers were in the barracks, but her and me. Consequently, I never considered myself a sociable person, due to being burnt too many times that I can even count. Especially, when it involved women or even allowed myself to be befriended by women. I was one, whom because of life experiences have become more selective or should I say meticulous about the female company that I allowed in my world. I felt this way simply, because many women are about drama.

Anyways, I was very reluctant to get involved with why she was crying more or less; truthfully, I didn't care. However, I began to think that maybe she had some children, whom like me were being left behind............which could be the reason she was crying, in the first place. Therefore, at least I could do, mother to mother thing which would be to lend an ear and/or give my support. Well, I guess, if she was a mother then part of me did care. So, I walked over and asked her, "Do you want to talk? Is there something I can help with?" That was when she said, "If I tell you, you have to promise me that you won't tell anyone." Although I knew at that moment, even if I said "I promised" that I knew depending on what the secret was that furthermore, I would not allow myself to become liable to a life and death situation.

Basically, at that point, it would be more about common sense and not about trying to keep a secret. Well, after I gave her my promise, she shared that she'd been having a sexual relationship with one of the senior staff............a SFC. Yes, [ding! ding! ding! ding!] remember I mentioned a few chapters back, in Chapter 5? Yes, my instincts about this platoon sergeant were right on point. Yes, and what do you know it, she shared that although she and this SFC were both married, they had been sexually involved; it has been ongoing for quite some time. Actually it began when they both attended a Unit summer activity, in Belize. She continued to report that things had been going great. According to her, he's been over her home many times, had spent the night and had even on occasions paid some of her bills.

O.K. That's her business. If she want to be involved with a married man, as well as be untrue in her own marriage, then that's on her. Why is she making this my business? Nevertheless, according to her, she noticed that just recently he'll become very controlling. When I inquired exactly what did she meant that he had become controlling? She reported that he'll become physically abusive and demanding. According to her, he had been wanting to know where she goes, who she's with, what time she's going to be home, and who's she's talking to on the phone; especially, when he's trying to call her and he can't get through the line.

OMG! If these weren't sure signs of an abusive relationship, then my name isn't "Yolanda." I knew these signs oh too well.......I too, had a history of being involved in relationships with abusive men. Whether it was verbal - emotional - physical or sexual. With regards to my past situations, it appeared that I had **"Abuse Me"** written across my forehead. So, although my experiences happened eight years ago, I thought I was already passed it................Apparently; it now became a fathom pain of remembrance. She explained that he has slapped, shoved, pushed, yelled, and grabbed her......... WAIT A MINUTE!!!!!!!!!!!!! Back Up!

Right about now, I'm sure you're wondering what I was thinking as well as, "Why was she allowing him to do that to her?" Well reader, that is a question, that only the one who is on the receiving end, can answer. Society can give their speculations, family and friends can be judgmental to say what they **coulda woulda, shoulda.** I am a true believer and from experience that no-one can say what they will or will not do until they have been placed in like or similar situation.............Let's move on, ...so much for my tangent..... There'll be more throughout this book, re: this female soldier, this SFC and my responses........

CHAPTER 8

First Injury; Raid Maneuvers at Fort Hood
&
Last Visit and Meal w/ Children-Family

Due to the level of danger that we were expected to face, in Iraq, raid maneuvers were pivotal for our training while at Fort Hood. During our training, every platoon was thereby separated in sections. Sometimes section one would be the good guys (US Soldiers), and section two was the enemy (Insurgents). As my section began running to take cover, my right hip took a blunt impact from a fall, when I dropped to a prone position. Because I was holding a leadership rank (SGT) and a female, I could not allow myself to show any pain. I could not allow myself to cry, although the pain was unbearable. What will my male counterparts say if they saw I was crying because I was injured?

Crying was not an option. Although, when the training was over, I tried to get up without showing any sign of pain. But, the pain over took my body, resulting in my inability to walk. I saw many of the soldiers, especially my male counterparts laughing and snickering that I was injured. I had felt that their laughing and snickering was very insensitive; to say the least. It made me begin to think that if we were in Iraq and in the war zone and I was injured, would these same soldiers stand by and laugh and snicker and say, "oh, she's just a female; she shouldn't be here." Those were the racing thoughts that I'd felt at that moment. Hence, I was immediately taken to TMC.

While at TMC, I was examined and provided an ice pack and Motrin. No consult for x-rays were recommended. And, although time has changed in allowing women to hold some of the same positions as men, as long if they are deemed fit to do so; we still have a long way to go with total equality for women in the military. Nevertheless, I continued to press forward with my injury, and not loosing time spent with my family when they visited.

During our last meal with our families, I enjoyed the moments spent with my children, uncle, mom and stepfather. I noticed my battle-buddy (Senior; Male-SSG who had a decorative history of serving in prior wars) was whisked away by my stepfather to talk. As they were away talking, I gave my children, uncle and mother a tour of my barracks. I later had a private talk with my children, letting them know how much I loved them and for them to respect their grandparents and to do well in school. Additionally, I wanted them to be careful who they associate with and to choose their friends wisely. I even told my son that I was not certain that I would be allowed to return for his high school graduation, but that his grandparents would be present, in my place. Hugs and kisses were exchanged, and I waved to my family as they drove away. Then I head to my barracks in preparation to receive additional instructions, and stand for formation.

As I returned to my barracks, the aura in the air was very dismal, as though, someone had just died. Sounds of the other female soldiers' cries amidst the air, had quickly spread throughout the barracks. I sat still for a moment, to let it all register. I then cried, then cried some more…………

I became even more afraid of the unknown of what is going to happen? I wanted so much for God to speak to me and tell me my future. What am I up against? Am I coming home in a body bag? Am I coming home mangled and without a limb? Will I still be able to function when I come home? What will I see? Will I be different? Will I be able to pick up from where I left off? When I return home, what's going to happen with my children? Will my children father take advantage of my situation and fight my parents in court to regain custody of my children? What if my children don't want to go? What if my son wants to go and my daughter doesn't?

Although I was reassured by my JAG Legal Advisor, re: my ex-husband trying to take advantage of my situation, by attempting to fight my parents in court for custody of my children, I could not help but worry and ask myself, "What are the laws of Texas, re: custody during deployment." I was shakened and at that moment, my mind was cloudy.............I cried and cried and cried some more, until I had no more tears to cry. A matter of fact, if I remember correctly, that was the last time I cried until I missed my son's high school graduation..........two months later.

CHAPTER 9

The Secret Taunted Me; I Hated to Look at Him
&
Boarding the Flight to Kuwait; Paradise - War (?)

As the days, weeks and months grew; I couldn't help but remember what was shared to me in confidence, back at Fort Hood. The secret taunted me, each time I heard his voice or saw his smirk, I just hated to look at him. The more I tried to distant myself from him; he continued to be in every place I turned. He had that annoying, scratchy-like voice that reflected at least 100-yards away. You knew when he entered the room. He had to make his presence known and if you were one, like me, who did not acknowledge him, he would make every attempt to inquire, "Is there a problem, Soldier?"

His demeanor to many was very intimidating excluding myself. Instead, he was transparent to me. I had his number (literally speaking). I've encountered men like him, before. I knew his angle and it wasn't working on me. Although, he made it very evident that he was God gift to women, by gloating about how good he looked. The smell of his distasteful cologne which he thought was appealing was awful. In March of 2004, as we boarded the flight to Kuwait, one of our fuel stops was in Switzerland. I remember this because I bought my son a Tommy Hilfiger watch and diamond studs as a graduation gift from one of the airport stores.

The weather was very brisk and the snow had covered the airport grounds. The flight was unquestionably very long. After our fuel stops, I slept the remaining of the flight. After arriving to Kuwait and settling in, I could not help to observe that the atmosphere was very peaceful. The weather was hot but very calm and the sand was very soft; like walking on the beach. Soldiers were walking around in PT (physical training) gear, socializing and laughing. Lines were long at the phone center, for soldiers waiting to call home, as well as, the lines to the fast food vendors.

I could not believe my eyes, in that, we had contracting vendors, i.e. Braums, Subway, Hardees, and one of the Pizza franchises (not for certain, which one). Wow, this was not "War"; this was paradise. All of a sudden, my negative thoughts and perception about the war had quickly diminished. I told myself, if this is war, I can do this, for I can do 1-1/2-2yrs of this with no problem. The tents were separated with males and females. My tent consisted of at least sixty females from various sister units, i.e. Alpha/Bravo/Charlie Co of the 980th Eng Battalion.

Time spent with this many women were very interesting. It was quite evident that not only were there a lot of estrogen floating around, but there were at least 50% of testosterone floating in the air. Yes, I said right. Testosterone.

Not all, but there were many who did not care, nor did they hide their sexuality, and many times were very blunt about it. Hey, whatever floats yours boat.....However; the problem I had was that, too often, there were times when these same female behaviors were observed to be very inappropriate for someone representing the United States uniform. As a woman, I began to feel very uncomfortable, especially when I was undressing. I always caught someone's eyes staring in my direction. As a result, I began getting undressed under my sleeping bag, or I would go out to the shower trailer or porter potty.

During the stay at Kuwait, my Platoon Sergeant (SFC; the individual who will be spoken about throughout this book) became even more obnoxious. SFC would for no reason at all, order his entire platoon to work out together; in the weight room. He made it appear that he was just wanting to stay in the know of where and what his soldiers were doing at all times. But, it wasn't at all that. His section consisted of about twelve male soldiers, and all of them were PFCs and SPCs except two at that time were SGT/SSG. Then, there were myself, the only female which due to a prior female SPC had remained stateside, because of family and personal issues. I found it to be very uncomfortable and could not understand how someone could have so much to talk about themselves, especially, about how women found him to be so attractive. OMG! This man was so into himself.

Anyway, after working out one evening and as I was returning to my sleep tent, SFC wanted to join me in the walk. During our walk, he began the conversation boasting about himself and his military accomplishments. Although, I could not forget what I had already knew about him; I was not at all impressed what he had to say. I remember him making a very arrogant statement, re: his awareness of women finding him attractive and how other male soldiers were envious of him." More and more as he spoke, I wanted to call him out and express how I really felt about him. But, he was my senior NCO, and I had a secret to keep.

We remained in Kuwait for about three months; setting up shop and work areas, until we were abruptly ordered to pack up and relocate. Intel was limited to only those who were privileged. Therefore, many of the lower ranking NCO's never knew what were going on, or what was on the agenda. Also, many times it made it very difficult to ease our discomfort, as well as, the discomfort of any lower enlisted soldiers, who may had been deployed straight out of basic training. Now, I was really worried..........Where were we going?

Phone/Communication Center

Outside View of the Female Tent in Kuwait

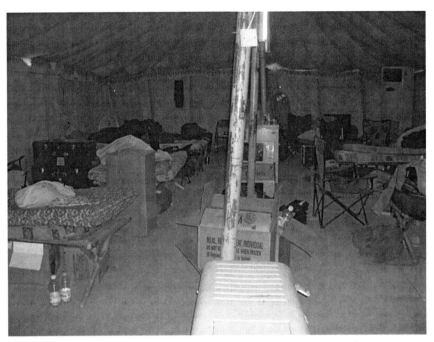

Inside View of the Female Tent in Kuwait)

CHAPTER 10

Traveling from Kuwait to Taji
&
The Wrong Turn

Our first mission was in Taji. Taji was a very disheveled city that lacked beatification. To clearly describe Taji, Taji was a place where many of the buildings had been demolished, due to attacks on the city. Much debris from the collapse buildings were observed everywhere and much of the debris were made into piles of trash; either from citizens in their country or from many of our military forces, using their equipments. Traveling into Taji was not a good experience. I remember the experience of leaving Kuwait; the travel appeared to be very long.

Although we all had our weapons ready to fire, the suspense, the not knowing, the quietness in the air was very discomforting............All I can remember saying to myself was, "Thank God the Iraqis were not equipped with airplanes to conduct air assaults." Nevertheless, another thought took over; in that, the Iraqis may not have access to conduct air assaults, but they sure is heck had access to the RPGs (Rocket Launcher) and Mortars, as well as the ability to use their informants to know which roads the military vehicles were traveling; in order to infiltrate a successful ambush.

Now, my fear really intensified. What was more discomforting was that this was the Unit Commanding Officer's first reported combat experience. Furthermore, his lack of communication skills with the NCOs was very poor. To think, this was a thirty-plus year old Commanding Officer who appeared to have difficulty listening, let alone communicating with his NCOs; especially those NCOS's whom this combat experience was nothing new to. A matter of fact, many of these Senior NCO's were known for having advanced and decorative experience of participating in previous war such as, the Gulf War. You would think, this Commanding Officer would have listened more to these NCOs. But he didn't. I don't know if it was his ego that would not allow him, or, if he just simply lacked communication skills. Whatever the reason, being under his direction was exactly that............."Direction", because it sure as heck wasn't "Leadership."

Hence, the travel appeared very long and no one was able to sleep. As the sun failed to shine its face, this was the time I relied on my eyes and ears, like never before. The roads and the streets were very dark. The only light reflection on the pavement was from the vehicles. The only noise heard, were from our vehicles. If we were planning an attack we would have been caught, just because of our loud vehicles.

As I began thinking about the noise level, I couldn't help but wonder how our military have been involved in so many wars, resulting in the lost of many of our men and women.

You would think that by now, with the help of modern technology, our military would be more equipped with silent air craft's and silent vehicles, to avoid easy attacks on our military forces.

Nevertheless, we took the wrong turn and by the orders given by the Commander. Although it was made clear by the Senior NCOs that the decision made by the Commander was incorrect, our driver along with the remaining of the convoy proceeded to take the wrong turn, in spite of following a direct order by the Commander.

After the wrong turn was made, if anyone were asleep, they were up now....Yes; we turned into a city that was very much alive and well. Many Iraqis began coming out of their homes. It appeared that my eyes may had been playing tricks on me, because it looked as though some of the Iraqis were holding, what appeared to be weapons and acting very suspiciously. The night quickly turned into day; although our convoy continued to travel through this unknown city. My mouth dropped and my heart was racing. Oh Lord, what now? Are we going to be ambushed, like the 507th? Is this it? Is this how I'm going to die? If so, at least my children will be proud of me and know that I was part of history and that I died so that they can live. The travel through that city was an ever ending journey. Although we eventually arrived safely in Taji, everyone was sleepy and tired. I began missing my children, even more. I began to wonder, what are they doing? Are they thinking about me? Are they sad that I'm not home? Are they mad with me, for re-enlisting?

Taking that wrong turn was a prime example of poor leadership. Poor leadership exists not only in the military, but it also spills over into the civilian sector. Too often, these individuals in management position believe that because they hold such titles that they earn the respect from their subordinates to follow direct orders. I have observed from first hand, this form of "Dictatorship" behavior being abused, more so in the private sector, only because these individuals generate their own Company Protocol and Operational Manual of how they want their employees to be controlled. In other words, you're simply being paid to be a puppet. You're told to come in and do your job; to shut up and don't say a word; don't provide any input. Yet, you say to yourself that you've gone to school, have advanced in your education, and you even have a vision where you see areas of improvement within the company to excel. Nevertheless, due to you're not the "right pick", the "right race", the "right color" or have the "right gene pool" or you don't have the "right connections" or you're not in the "right click" or you're simply not in with the "elite" then, you don't have a voice.

It has been shown that following direct orders by those in leadership, without using one's own common sense has costed many lives. Holding a title doesn't make one any smarter or more knowledgeable... ....It only highlights one's advancement in education, not so much one's life experience which can be the cherry on a cake. Since my return from Iraq, not only has it been an ongoing challenge, but it has been a daily trigger for me to work under novice management.

These are individuals who don't have a clue about the first thing about leading anyone; let alone managing a staff. Yes, they desire the title.......ok ...yet, they turn the responsibility into a Dictatorship, by intimidating and building a hostile work environment, instead of learning how to motivate their staff with positive incentives. Remember, respect is earned **NOT** given. **YOU HAVE TO LEAD BY EXAMPLE!** Try, listening to your staff and be **PROACTIVE** before jumping to be REACTIVE!

Dishelved City in Taji, Iraq

Another View of the Dishelved City in Taji, Iraq

Taking the Wrong Turn; Traveling Through the Unidentified City

Another View of Traveling Through the Unidentified City

SOLUTION:
A way to help build a company or agency moral is: Place a suggestion box out in an accessible area to the staff. The purpose of the suggestion box is so that the staff can enter their suggestions; anonymously, of changes they wish to see within the company, as well as within management. During management staff meeting, all the suggestions should be viewed; however 1x a week 1 suggestion should be approved.

CHAPTER 11

Not Being Present for my Son's Graduation
&
The Start of Becoming Mentally Unbalanced

Since the beginning of arriving in Taji, there appeared to be ongoing explosions; attacks by rockets. Although I was not old enough to join the military, during Vietnam, but hearing reports from my late uncle; as well as, other current Vietnam friends/Veterans; I could only vision the similar smoke from left over explosions that amidst the air or the sound that radiated from the RPG's. Day in and day out, rockets continued landing in our locations. Nevertheless, time after time our unit and soldiers had to continue to take position for immediate cover, due to any possible airborne shrapnel's. Although time after time, I continued thinking about my son's graduation, a precious moment that no mother can get back, once missed. My flat effect became evident to other soldiers. I became very disconnected. Many times I felt as though I was physically present, but mentally, I was all over the place. I began to suffer with physiological symptoms, as well as depressive symptoms; i.e. stomach discomfort, loss of appetite and inability to sleep.

Furthermore, this SFC did not make it easy with his annoying and arrogant presence. Even though I continued and kept my military barren, executed as ordered, as well as kept a secret that had now begun to trigger my past domestic abuse. Hence, I began to dread the nights, because I knew I had to sleep and was afraid to close my eyes. My sleep began to become effected. My sleep turned into mental torture. I began thinking about the first six months of my marriage in 1986, to my children father, who was a former Corporal in the United States Army. I remembered my ex-husband had been drinking earlier that afternoon. It was a Saturday evening and I was talking back to him.

Immediately, he grabbed me by my neck and threw me onto the couch and began choking me. My son was nine months old; I thought I was going to die. I had begun to see silver specks floating around in my eyes. Thus, I could not breathe.....He then let up. I was in shock. I couldn't believe what just happened.

Did this man (my ex-husband) just choke me? No, that didn't just happen. I'm sure, he won't do it again. He was just a little tipsy. Maybe if I didn't upset him, he would not have become angry with me and done what he did. He did it because he was drunk. I don't believe that he meant to hurt me. Yes, I had excuses for his behavior. And, all these questions and statements were floating around in my mind; after that episode. After all, I was raised by my paternal grandmother and had always heard her tell my aunts, "You stand by that man, no matter what."

As a child, raised by my paternal grandmother, I witnessed and experienced domestic violence on a daily basis, especially when family members were intoxicated, which was daily. Being of a Native Indian descendent [Cherokee], consumption of alcohol for my paternal family was the norm. There were no tolerance levels when it came to the consumption of alcohol. I remember hearing my grandmother tell one of my aunts, whom was always fighting with her husband, "no matter what, you stay with your husband; because, if he hit you, you must of done something to pist him off." Wow; in the defense of the man.

Nevertheless, this was embedded in me from the beginning of my innocent years. So, I remained married and was too ashamed to tell my mother or the maternal family, whom were of the Irish descendent. Nervously, I knew had I told my mother's side of the family, no doubt, they would have come to my rescue and there would have been a bloody war. So, go figure....I am an African American mixed with Native [Cherokee] Indian and Irish. Anyways, my maternal families were very family oriented people and the women were well respected, opposed to my paternal family. But the question was....Why was I now, remmemnancing on something that had happened over ten years ago? Apparently, I had begun to internalize this female soldier's secret. It was taunting me. Her physical abuse and secret had now become a trigger for me. Should I tell? But, it is her secret. Resentfully, it was her business.

However, nights in Iraq continue to grow even longer. I then began reminiscing about a second incident, in 1991. My ex-husband relocated me and the children to Illinois, after being displaced from work, due to being placed on workman's comp; following a neck and back injury from an head on collision with another eighteen-wheeler. I remember this day as though it was yesterday. I had just enrolled in a local Junior Community College. My major was Criminal Justice. I had dreams to one day pursue a Law Degree. As I arrived home from school, I began sitting on the living couch (yes, the couch incident, again) to begin my homework. My ex-husband had been out all day and driven to Chicago with his brother and uncle; as a result he arrived home hungry and wanted to know why I had not cooked; at least, prepared him a sandwich. Nevertheless, I told him that I was trying to finish my homework and since he was already in the kitchen, he could prepare himself a sandwich. He then asked, "What did you say?" At this point, I sensed that he had been drinking and using drugs, while he was out with his relatives, because that was the lifestyle they kept.

He waited awhile after his family left. Soon after they left, he asked me again why I hadn't prepared dinner. Suddenly, because I did not repeat myself and I remained focused on my school work, to avoid any confrontation, he walked into the living room, threw my books out of my hand, grabbed me by my feet and dragged me off the couch, from the living room, through the den; thereby, opening the front door and threw me out the door. He then locked the door behind me; so that I could not regain entry. There, I stood outside in the snow with no shirt or blouse on, just in my bra and jeans, in twenty degree weather.

I could now hear my children, ages one and a half and five years old crying. They had been awakened by the noise. They were yelling and screaming for him to let me in. I then was able to hear him threaten the children that if they didn't go to bed that he would beat their [blank], then throw them outside with me. With every attempt, I tried to enter the house; by climbing on some cement bricks, in order to crawl through the window on the side of the house. Unfortunately, he caught me and quickly slammed the window down, almost catching my fingers. Since he had locked the windows, I wasn't able to gain entry.

Hence, I couldn't get into the house, I just sat in the freezing cold, and I sat on the front steps, with only my jeans and bra, until he decided to open the door. Throughout the night, I said nothing. Stiffened with anger, I was thinking of the movie, "The Burning Bed"; with Farah Fawcett, and how could I kill this man and not serve time for it? How could I poison him and get away with it? Then, I began to think about my children.
What may have worked back then, wouldn't work now, because of the many available resources for Victims of Domestic Violence. Besides, he wasn't worth serving prison time for. Therefore, the next day while he was out gallivanting with his brother and while the children were in daycare, I walked to a nearby telephone booth to telephone the police.

The dispatch then transferred me to speak to someone from a local domestic violence shelter. I was given explicit instructions on how to remain safe, and how to leave my husband. Next, I went home, packed two large suitcases of mine and my children clothes and toy, and slid them under the bed [The bed that my ex-husband and I slept].

On the second day, same routine occurred, but this time, I left my children at the local police department, I requested an escort to return to my home, to gather our suitcases which were stashed under the bed. My ex-husband never suspected the suitcases under the bed. Why would he? He never swept or mopped under the bed. Abuse me once, shame on you; abuse me twice shame on me........Therefore, that was the end of the abuse from the hands of my ex-husband and I never looked back. Although, I was able to have the strength and the courage to walk away from the abuse of my husband, it's recorded that there are many women who aren't fortunate. As a result, many women and their children are killed, before they decide to leave.......................But again, why was this female soldier's secret affecting me to this level of magnitude?

My son's graduation was slowly approaching. I recalled a while back, requesting to attend my son's graduation, however, I was informed that I needed to have been physically in theatre for at least six months before any R&R would be granted. Yet, the first group of soldiers that were granted R&R went home two or three days before the date of my son's graduation. Finally, I was offered in place of another soldier. Of course, I declined the offer, because I knew that I would have still arrived a few days after my son's graduation.

Reluctantly, many of my calls and emails to my son went unanswered and even when he was at home; he was too busy to come to the phone. It didn't take a rocket scientist to figure out that my son was angry. He was first angry that I re-enlisted. He made that apparent, during our last face to face conversation. Secondly, he was angry that I wouldn't be present for his Senior Walk. Third, I wouldn't be present for his Prom. Forth, I wouldn't be present for his graduation and Finally, I wouldn't be present for his first enrollment in college. Wow, this was a lot for a mother to miss. The pain wouldn't had been so unbearable, if I had been married or was in a healthy relationship. I later received a package from my stepfather; it was a DVD of the ceremony of my son's high school graduation. I lost it; I could not hold back my tears. I wanted so much to be in attendance. My son will never know how I truly felt. His anger had clouded him, which had blocked me out.

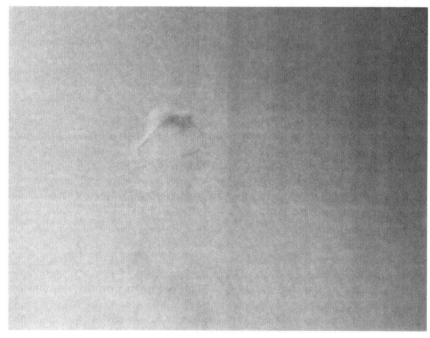

Air Aftermatch Explosion

CHAPTER 12

Camp Striker-Victory: The Secret is Revealed
&
Internal Investigation

We were now at our second location. Camp Striker-Victory was to many soldiers the place to be, because there were more activities, eateries; similar to Kuwait. Remember a few chapters back, I mentioned of another female soldiers who was crossleveled to our platoon? Well, due to family and personal reasons she remained stateside. Therefore, when we arrived to this camp I was assigned my own sleeping quarters (one-man tent). Of course I didn't have any problems with that, especially since I was cross leveled from another Unit and considering many of the lifestyles and the behaviors I had already observed, I clearly did not feel as though I belong, anyway.

A matter of fact, from here out, since I was the only female in my Platoon, I was always assigned my own sleep quarters. Except once, when I had to share a tent with my entire male platoon, due to the sleep tents were given away to another branch of service or another platoon. Honestly, I don't quite remember the specifics why I had to share a tent with my platoon. However, I can only speculate, which will be briefly discussed in the latter of the chapters. Anyway, let's not digress. Here's where more reports of abuse were compiled onto the previous secret. It was one late evening, in May 2004 [It was Mother's Day] and many of the soldiers were out of their tents, either at the gym or at the activity center (I forgot the name of it) when the abuse occurred.

My tent was an adjoining tent with other senior male NCOs (SSGS), but, they too were not in. This female soldier (SSG) came to my tent, once again crying. She asked, "Was there anyone else here?" I said no. I couldn't help but notice that she was very upset and crying and I had a clue as to why. Therefore, I called it like I saw it and asked, "What the.... [blank]......did he do to you, Now?" She began crying, even more. She then said that she went to his tent to try to end their relationship, but he wouldn't let her leave. According to her report, he told her that he didn't want her to leave him. Also, if he couldn't have her, then he didn't want any other man to have her. She continued to report that a struggle took place, which resulted in her being slapped and grabbed by her wrist. You (writer) are probably asking, "Well, how did I know her story was legit?"

Well, although she was of dark complexion, she had a visible hand print to her face, as well as, marks on her wrist that appeared to be marks from a struggle. Then I inquired of her, "Why won't he let you out of the relationship?" Her response was, "because he said he loves me and that soon after he file for his divorce that we were going to be together."

Apparently, SFC was currently separated from his wife and children. My guess was, because of similar issues ......explosive and out of control anger episodes. Hmm, does Manic Mood Disorder ring a bell? Hold that thought, because later in this book this premature diagnosis will be revisited. I then asked if she wanted me to go with her to report him? However, she declined; although her reason had some logic.

According to her, there were many strikes against them both, which could result in them both getting in a lot of trouble............. First, although they both were separated from their spouses, due to marital discord, they were still legally married. Secondly, they both were senior NCOs (SSG / SFC). They are supposed to lead by example. Isn't that part of the NCOs creed? Third, there was no fraternizing allowed; although, there were many soldiers fraternizing, but more so, many married couples. As I continued to talk with her, I found it to be very interesting how she appeared more concerned about what "he" was up against to lose, opposed to herself.

She began to explain that she was worried that if anyone discovered their involvement, that he may lose his chances of retirement/benefits and/or even get demoted. What! Are You Serious? O..........k. At that moment I began to think, being a survivor of domestic violence; I couldn't fathom why she was so concerned about him and his loses. Could there have been more to what she was not saying? What was the real motive to staying with him? What was her real angle? Could it be, if his retirement and benefits were compromised, the fear that she'll end up with a man with nothing? No money? This could also dampen on her parade, of not being able to keep up with her high maintenance lifestyle of no more pedicures / manicures/body waxes and weave? Come on, let's get real............

This man is slapping you, choking you, grabbing at you and you're worry about the upkeep of your high maintenance lifestyle? This sounds ludicrous. I told her that I couldn't continue to allow her to confide in me, and not do anything about it. Therefore, I asked her not to confide in me, no longer. I wasn't going to be an accomplice if this man ends up killing her or she snap and shoot this man with her M-16. No, I didn't want to know anymore. Although, I had already been tainted with the information that was already confided in me.

As days, weeks and even months had gone by I tried to continue performing my duties. I was a Sergeant, my title was an Automatic Logistic Specialist; assigned to the motor pool. As an ever ending task, the majority of my duties while in Iraq were overseeing the supply inventories of the vehicles, as well as responsible for transporting vehicles, radios and weapons to various warehouse depots in Iraq, for repair. During the evenings, there were times I secured check points and tower guard duties, in watch of incoming/ongoing enemy attacks.

If I remember correctly, because SFC was so controlling and wanted to look good in the eyes of the First Sergeant and the Commander that our Platoon was subjected to several unnecessary platoon meetings, which interfered with our personal time. Such as, writing letters, calling and emailing families, etc. Yet, I kept my composures.

But of course, he wasn't concerned about his personal time of writing letters to his family back at home, because, it was apparent that he was too busy trying to control the female soldier(s), and attempting to build a family, while in Iraq. Go figure..........Many times, he basically repeated himself about the next day assignments which had already been communicated by his senior NCOs. Also, he was always exhuming this sense of grandiose attitude, he didn't allow himself to see that anyone could actually execute what was instructed. He was so into himself, that he didn't believe that he was replaceable. Plus, one thing I've learned over the years that we're all replaceable. There's always someone who's better and more intelligent...........no one is untouchable or invincible.

But to SFC..........hmm, to him, he thought he was the "[S.....]"! Besides, after awhile, he sensed that I wasn't a female that was going to drool over him; neither did I find him attractive. A matter of fact, he was not my flavor of coffee. Therefore, I avoided him like people avoid skunks. I especially didn't allow myself to be alone, in his presence. He was someone whom couldn't be trusted. He reminded me so much of the snake in the Garden of Eden; as he slithered his way into the minds of the Commanding Officers, and the hearts of many female soldiers who found him to be irresistible. Yes, would you believe this SFC had two married SSGs fighting over him (literally). And, for what? The more I'd to work with this platoon sergeant, the more I felt uneasy, angry, disconnected, repressed hatred and unfocused on my duties. Honestly, I had to ask myself, if SFC was on fire, would I even want to waste my spit, to spit his way?

Therefore, while on my lunch break, I took a walk to visit the local Chaplin. I could no longer carry this female soldier's secret and manage my own monsters (triggers/nightmares), as well as feeling depressed, and due to the loss relationship with my son.

I was becoming someone I didn't know. How does one function, in the midst of carrying someone else's burdens? I'm not God, for he carried the burden of the world. He hung and died for us all. Could I've truly said that if SFC was hit by shrapnel that I would help by, administering immediate medical attention until he was able to be airvac, for a higher level of care? Or would I simply just walk away, and let him bleed to death? I was beginning to question my morals. Yes, he was an evil man who deserved to be punished, but did he deserve for me to turn my back on him, if it really came to it?

Would I really be able to? Should I? Could I? I needed to let go of this secret, and then focus on my own issues. So I did, but before I left, the Chaplin asked if he and his assistance could pray for me that I would have peace. So, they did. I couldn't help neither, was I able to hold back my tears. Therefore, The Unit location and demographics were provided to the Chaplin to speak to the appropriate personnel, in order to begin an internal investigation.

Honestly, the look on this Chaplin's face seemed to be, one, who may have known someone, such as a loved one, who may have been subjected to domestic violence. For, I felt his sincerity. In addition, I know the tears that I shed wouldn't undue the permanent scars left behind for any victims of domestic violence. Yes, we may forgive, but how do we forget. Can you? Should you? Should We?

Night Tower Guard Duty

Ouside View of my Individual Sleep Tent

Scarred, but not Broken

Inside View of my Sleep Tent

CHAPTER 13

A Disgrace to God/Family/Uniform/Country
&
Convoys; a Repercussion Measure

After my visit with the Chaplin, it appeared as though it was less than a few hours that my Commander and First Sergeant were updated on my visit and report. An investigation took place, and other soldiers were called in and questioned about their knowledge of SFC/SSG's ongoing affair. Although the many soldiers reported overtime to present what they have observed, even with regards to the abuse, this female SSG denied everything. Yes, you read right. She denied everything. Not only did she deny everything, but so had he. Well of course, she wasn't respected thereafter by any of the soldiers who were called, to give their report. Many of the soldiers, including myself were very disappointed and upset, because we jeopardized our ranks and military careers to advocate in her defense. As for SFC, he walked away without a spot or blemish.

As for me................let's just say, because she denied any abuse, I now became that spot on the wall, the big "X" on my back, the zit that teenagers try to avoid the night before a date. Why? Because SFC had for so long been able to cover his tracks and come out spotless. She feared him. She'd prior been threatened by him, for he knew where she lived and he knew where she worked. More importantly, he knew she'd had a weakness for him. He always had soldiers, both senior and lower enlisted, as well as officer's on his payroll (literally speaking), in a way of, you wash my back, I'll wash yours......you do for me and, I'll hook you up. Quid pro Quo.

This was observed to be normal behavior for this Unit. From day one, I observed the misuse and undocumented supplies being distributed. Well, after this investigation I continued to be ostracized, even by the male soldiers in my platoon.

Did anyone care, but me? Or was it because I was the only one with a history of being a survivor of domestic violence. Did they just see me as a survivor scorned? For once, I wanted to be that voice. Not just for this SSG, but I wanted to be a voice for all victims of domestic violence, everywhere. How did everyone now see me? For one, I was not a soldier initially assigned to their Unit, anyway; so, did they see me as someone coming in, trying to mess up a good thing, for them? A trouble maker?

Hence, it was evident that the investigation left a bad taste in the mouths of the First Sergeant/Commander and other Officers which resulted in me, thereafter being called and interrogated on a daily basis. Day in and day out I was being interrogated, more so by the First Sergeant. Apparently, it was obvious that the First Sergeant and SFC were "buddy-buddy." They both had been assigned to the Unit for quite some time. Opposed to the commander, he, like me and other soldiers had been crossleveled.

I felt isolated and alone. Very Alone. I felt as though I was fighting a losing battle. No one wanted to be seen around me, let alone, allowed to talk to me which was by direct order from the First Sergeant. I recall being told by one of the male soldiers that the First Sergeant had ordered that no one is to be caught communicating with me and if they were caught, they would get in trouble.

What? Am I the only one who realized that we're still at war; yet, I'm being singled out and soldiers are being threatened by this First Sergeant about socializing with me. Are you serious? Am I missing something, here? What is it that I'm missing or just not seeing? These officials and NCOs were a total disgrace to the uniform. Things escalated. Furthermore, as a repercussion measure to "keep my mouth closed"; as the First Sergeant put it, I was thereafter placed on dangerous convoys.

O......k, unless this First Sergeant was afraid that I knew some information about him, that could ruin his military career, but what was it? What was it that he was afraid that I knew that he wanted me to keep my mouth closed about?

Anyways, there were many times I had no idea that I was going out on a convoy; until the last minute when my name was called during roll call. Were they trying to scare me? If so, I had already come to peace with my God, if should this be my way to leave this earth. I had nothing to lose. I no longer had a relationship with my son. As for my daughter, she was being taken care of by her grandparents. Furthermore, I wasn't leaving behind a spouse. I didn't have a dog, I didn't care for cats, and birds were too messy to care for .... And, I'd simply become numb. So, I wasn't going to break. And, each time they sent me out on convoys, I prayed to my God: "Lord, you know what's going on. You see what they're doing to me. I have no more strength to fight. You see what I am up against. Let my children know, I died for a cause greater than myself." However, with every convoy................. I became even more numb.

CHAPTER 14

Racism; Yes, It Still Exist; Even in the Military
&
The War inside the War, Between the U.S. Military Branches;
"We're better; No, We're better"

Remember, at the latter of Chapter 5, I mentioned about a soldier who I referred to speak to Legal about a racial incident? Well, this was that soldier. Now, to think I already allowed myself to be the voice of someone who was a victim to domestic violence. Yet, I now had a male soldier, promoted to a SPC, reporting to me that he'd been subjected to racism in his tent. Yes, you read right. Nevertheless, before I share his story, I'm sure you're (Reader) wondering, why are these soldiers confining in me. That was a question I've always asked myself. For some apparent reason, people have always been drawn to confide in me; which was the reason after this deployment, I later pursued a Master's Degree in Counseling.

This was a Mexican male soldier, who was also the Commander's personal assistance/driver. I mentioned back in Chapter 5 that he was requesting his Government Driver License, because he was assigned to be the Commander's Driver' while in Iraq. Also, I mentioned that this same soldier ended up being one of my Angels, during my deployment in Iraq. Anyway, he reported that day in and day out he have been subjected to racial connotations, by the other Caucasian male soldiers whom he shared a tent with. If I remember correctly, his initial complaint was that those soldiers hung Hitler's Swastikas and used the words "Niggers, Spit and Cunt" and made negative and racial statements with regards to him being assigned as the Commander's personal Driver.

Now, how I became involved was that this soldier knew that I had a criminal justice background, (AS and BS in Criminal Justice). Since, I'd been crossleveled from a JAG unit, as well as had access to my MCM (Manual for Courts Martial Edition), he felt comfortable to come to me for advice. Clearly, I informed him that it was pure racism and I suggested that he report and address his concerns to Legal, which, he did. Although, of course another investigation took place. Everything was fine, so I thought, until the First Sergeant discovered that I had something to do with advising this soldier to go to Legal. Even though swastikas were discovered hanging in this soldier's tent, by the soldiers in questioned; from my knowledge, these soldiers only received a slap on the wrist. As for me, it was round two with the interrogation from the First Sergeant and the Commander. Thus, this time, it was even more humiliation and never ending emotional and verbal torture.

The first Sergeant ordered me to report to his office and without my battle buddy or squad leader present. When I arrived, the First Sergeant was present, as well as the Commander.

As I stood at ease, the First Sergeant paced back and forth yelling; even making sly jokes that I wanted to be an in-house lawyer, like in the prisons [then, they both laughed]. On the contrary, I stood there for about ten to fifteen minutes, it seemed as though I was standing there for at least thirty minutes, if not more; while they both laughed and gallivant in my face. Not once, did I shed a tear, for I knew what this was all about. It wasn't that I helped a soldier file a valid complaint against racism. No, what this was really about was that I was actually exhibiting the true leadership qualities of an NCO. I was leading by example. I knew I'd done no wrong. I was in no violation. I was taking care and advocating for a soldier. Most importantly, I wasn't compromising my integrity. Yes,

Scarred, but not Broken

that's what this was really about. They couldn't comprehend how a woman could be this smart and this fierce and not blink a eye. Although, I couldn't understand how they were being so insensitive to something as powerful as "**racism / discrimination.**"................

Hence, before I was being allowed to leave, the First Sergeant stated, "SGT Jones, I'm going to be watching you, wherever you go and whatever you do, I will be right there. You think you're smart; you ought to mind your business and keep your nose out of where it doesn't belong, you're excused." Wow, if I wasn't mistaken, that sounds a bit similar to something that would have been said back in the 1940's to some African American traveling to the south from the north; inquiring about why race isn't treated fairly abroad; the same in the South as it's in the North. Hmmm.......Well, it was apparent that his true color was showing itself. Furthermore, it was also apparent that racism continued throughout this deployment.

Either I was naive or I just wasn't aware that racism still existed, even in today's military. How could there still be racism, especially after all these years and after all these past wars? My mind began racing and I began thinking. How could I trust that the Caucasian male or female soldier standing beside me was going to have my back, if we were ambushed? Was he or she going to stop and think......... "Hmm, wait a minute, I can't help SGT Jones, because what will my people back home say? What are they going to think when they read in the papers?"

The Tuskegee Airmen is a good example of breaking the barriers to racism in the military. The Tuskegee Airmen were the first Black Airmen, during the World War II who shot down many enemy planes in support for the war; to protect our Country. Their story will forever be a monument of how they were subjected to racism, stateside and overseas, even after their heroic deed. It is apparent, that racism in the military is still **alive and well**.

I also recalled being assigned to work with another unit while in Iraq. The person of contact was a Caucasian male NCO of whom was caught many times making subtle racist remarks about some of the African American soldiers shaped heads, features and their lips. This NCO and I butt heads, more times than I can remember because, I may have been a woman of color, but, I wasn't going to back down from him neither, was I intimidated by him.

This NCO would deliberately make smart comments about my shaved head, as a provoking measure to get a response from me. Yes, I did a GI-Jane prior, of being deployed. I shaved my head because, I wasn't trying to go over to Iraq to make a fashion statement, or to look cute or even to pick up a man. Beside, who was I going to sit down to break bread with during time of war? Anyways, I was going to war. I took on the war attitude. I wanted to blend in with my soldiers, my male counterparts. I did not want, neither, did I expect to be treated special just because I was a woman. I wanted to be treated, as an equal. More importantly, I wanted my male counterparts to know that when the chips dropped, they would be able to count on me, tampon, migraines, PMS and all. I had their back.

Furthermore, going back to this NCO. When I did respond to this NCO's inquiries, my responses were never that of someone who wasn't able to articulate, but they were responses that always left him standing with his mouth dropped and of course looking stupid, which often burnt him to the bones. I remembered clearly, he made a comment in how impressed he was about me using "proper grammar" ……What the… [blank]…..
Trust me, that was exactly what I wanted to say. But, you know, I truly feel sorry for people who still have this slave mentality, regardless of what race they are; whom generalize all African Americans and believe that all African Americans doesn't have the ability to articulate or excel. What is even more appalling is when African Americans tear down other African American; just because they want to remain in bondage and do not want to excel, themselves. Sorry, I digressed a little and went on a tangent……..

But, what's even sadder is that, the majority of these uninformed individuals lack a higher education, themselves; hence providing more and more opportunities for African Americans, as well as other minorities groups to continue to surpass in the areas of Higher Education. Nevertheless, my responses no longer upset him. Instead, he became intrigued by me which later resulted in him making sexual advances towards me. Was he serious? Yes, apparently he was. Consequently, when he saw that I wasn't going to give in one way, he decided to take another approach. His continuous racial and sexual advances added to making my stay in Iraq a living hell on earth. Each day that I had to work with this man and see his face, I felt as though this man was undressing me with his eyes.

As I would pass him, he would make frequent attempts to try to brush up against me; even though his counterparts were watching and said nothing; but laughed which resulted in day to day brawls and verbal altercations between him and me. And, although I reported my concerns to his senior NCO, my voice went unheard. And, of course I was not able to go to my own First Sergeant or Commander, because they were already putting me through hell, too. However, I did many times confide in my battle buddy #1 (SSG) as well as, my battle buddy/Angel #2. They, at least tried to protect me, by periodically stopping by to visit me in my work area.

For, they knew that this NCO was in my work area and he would always find an excuse just to be physically close to me.

After awhile, I no longer had any protection, because he would complain to his senior NCO and Commander that soldiers from my Unit were frequently coming by and distracting me from working. OMG! He was such a liar and a manipulator. He only said that to keep me to himself. For a brief moment, I thought I was reliving the life of my ancestors, back in the 1800 working on a plantation. Instead of working out in the field, I was kept in the house like many of the light complexion in-house slaves. More and more and day after day, I dreaded not only working with this NCO, but just being in Iraq. I really felt so dirty after working all day with this man. Yes, I felt violated, even without any sexual body fluids being exchanged (Metaphorically speaking). As a result, I began to think about how much I was missing my children and wanted to be with them, more than anything. At least with my children I knew their love was real and they appreciated me.

Hasn't racism gone on long enough? Better yet, help me understand something. Didn't Abraham Lincoln sign the Emancipation Proclamation on January 1, 1863 during the American Civil War, declaring that all persons held as slaves within the rebellious states shall be made free? So, isn't slavery over? And, at what point does racism cease? Hasn't there been enough innocent blood shed? What's the problem? Are we ever going to get it right?

If the racism wasn't enough; if the sexual harassment wasn't enough; if the secret of the physical abuse/assault wasn't enough; if missing my son's graduation wasn't enough; if being intentionally placed on convoys wasn't enough; if being threatened/shunned wasn't enough; if being in Iraq wasn't enough; then, there were the war inside the war between the branch of services. This needs to be addressed. Yes, although I am guilty of this with regards to joking with my veteran friends at the local VA, around a cup of coffee that is one thing. But, when the treatments of the branches aren't spread equally, it's what causes the rife between the branches of services. Too often I've observed the Army having the last pick with regards to sleeping quarters, and/or the last to eat for chow.

Many times we slept in worst condition, opposed to other branch of services. I remember sleeping in tents that were leaking from the ceiling, or tents without any A/C or Heat. Yet, other branches were living in better conditions. Basically, it balls down to this, one branch of service believing that their better than the next or one branch of service striving to get more recognition for their service, than the other. This is nothing new; according to my seniors in my family and prior War Veterans whom I share coffee with, down at the local VA (Veteran Hospital). This war between branches of services has been ongoing, before I was born. When does it stop? We are all supposed to be fighting for the same cause.........

July 2, 2004   22:35

We need to nuke all these ~~Fagots~~ MF They are stupid MF that can not hook up shit.

Are we suppose to have someone from maintenance here? ▇▇▇▇. I rather have him than some of the MF at least we can deal with him better he's just gay

IF I could drive the Commander and be in air Condition tent. I'll be alright

Why can't we just stay with Americans Why can't it be a white girl.

By the year 2010 Texas will be the only state that whites will be Considered a minority. The Fucken Mexicans will be taken over.

How many doctors talk correct English you can't even understand them

CHAPTER 15

Not Easily Intimidated; To Be a Woman - African American & Educated
&
Gambling/Drugs/Prostitution/Rapes/Adultery

There were many strikes against me from the start, being crossleveled with this Unit. For one, apparently this unit wasn't ready for me. They were not ready for an African American woman who wasn't easily intimidated who had a strong personality and educated. I wasn't one who boasted in what I knew. Instead, I allowed my actions to speak for itself. I guess I can say, life experiences molded me to be who I'd become, prior to being deployed. I wasn't going to surrender, without a good fight. I was a fighter, even before the deployment, both mentally and physically. For, I'd learned from the very best about maintaining focused and balanced with the universe through Ki Energy.

Prior to being deployed, I graduated to a High Red Belt in Tae Kwon Do. However, before being honored to wear the High Red Belt, I learned during my Red Belt phase about transforming Ki or Vital Energy (cosmic ocean; basic bioenergy) to obtain perfect balance. Hence, the art of Tae Kwon Do does not separate the mind and body; instead, the balance exists between the physical- emotional and intellectual. The red belt signified the color of blood or sun; while, developing a strong foundation of the body and nature. But most importantly, I learned from this art and at this level of phase the codes of "Loyalty - Respect - Honesty and Standing for

Justice." That is exactly what I set out to do, during my deployment experience. Although, it was not welcomed. Instead, it was meant with continuous verbal attacks by the Commander and First Sergeant.

Apparently, my mission to do what was honorable and justice was not acceptable. Basically, my presence and my voice had begun to rain on their parades. Meaning, I no longer believed that I was at war with another country; in order to protect my own and my loved ones in the rear. No, I began to question the reason for even being in Iraq. Had I gotten caught up and been invited to the Devil's stomping ground? Yes, you read right. Everywhere I turned, there were inappropriate behavior from both men and women, that had they been state side their behaviors would have warranted an arrest. Yes, from gambling, prostitution, to drug drugs being bought by some of the local Iraqis and sold to many of the soldiers. I'm not only referring to some of the soldiers in the Unit that I was deployed with; but I'm also referring to many of the soldiers who were deployed from other Units and countries abroad.

Coming from a blood line of family War Veterans, as well as having Veteran colleagues from the Vietnam era; many of their stories are very consistent and very sad and heartened to hear. And, although we lost many to the Vietnam War, the Vietnam War was not our War to fight, in the first place. Some may disagree, others may not. However, I'm sure we all can agree that rape is never acceptable nor is it ever justifiable at anytime; whether, it is the rape against the enemy or the rape against our own. Nevertheless, the rapes on many Vietnamese Women and young girls, during Vietnam weren't a justifiable cause. Apparently, nothing has changed, with regards to our so-call "GI's and how many of them viewed women.

Whether, the women are in uniform or out of uniform. However, in my case, the tables were turned. This time, the women that were being bear- hugged and raped and left without any clothing on their bodies were US Female Soldiers, by Yes! Few of our own US males in uniform. It was difficult enough being a woman in today's military; let alone a long time waiting to finally be accepted as a woman into the military. Although, our military have come a long way in accepting women into the ranks, it still became difficult to be away from home and to know that "we" (US female soldiers) couldn't trust, nor were we even safe from our own that were in uniform.

At first we were able to walk to the shower trailers alone. Then, to add insult to injury, females were being kidnapped and raped and left naked; not to have known what and who had kidnapped them, because of blacking out. Soon after, females were instructed to walk in pairs. Well, after awhile the assailants began to travel in groups, which resulted in the female pairs were kidnapped and raped, as well. Thereafter, it became very unsafe for any females to go anywhere on the installation alone; without the escort of the male soldiers from their assigned Units to stand guard outside the shower doors. The rapes had now been elevated to High Alert!!!!! Well, if we couldn't trust our own and we couldn't trust the local Iraqis, then who could "we" trust, while representing the uniform and our country? **WHO WAS PROTECTING US?** Something has to stop! We can't continue to allow our male soldiers to misrepresent the uniform and misuse of their ranks and getting out of control, **War after War after War!**

The only difference in the soldiers behaviors during my deployment in Iraq; opposed, to the behaviors that were expressed in Vietnam was the **change in venue**. It's apparent, just like I didn't just awaken and suddenly experienced domestic violence flash backs. No, I had a history of domestic violence, prior to joining the military. Although, I don't recall there ever being a place on my entry application that it ask if I've ever been a victim to spousal abuse. Same rains true for these men who join the military with possible **Sexual Assaults, Narcissistic and Bipolar Disorder** backgrounds, yet they slipped through the cracks.

Another behavior that was so prevalent and observed throughout this deployment was, adultery/infidelity. Whatever name or word to describe a legally married person who behaves in an unfaithful manner that may be consistent of sexual connotations - sexual misrepresentation with another, whom isn't their spouse. Listen, that man or that woman doesn't' belong to you, it's "Plain and Simple." I can speak, because I am no angel, for I have some skeletons in my closets, too. Especially, in my past of vulnerability while I was experiencing spousal abuse. We're all human, but the moral to it all is, admitting and owning up to it. Then, doing what's right. That's why I can talk, and I can be that voice to advocate for others, who want to do the right thing.......

That married man is lying, and he isn't leaving his wife for you. If he's cheating on his wife with you, then he's going to cheat on you with someone else. Don't sell yourself cheap. Your jewels are worth more than what he has to offer. [Same things apply to you men. She isn't worth it. That married woman is lying, for she isn't leaving her husband for you. Just like you're trying to be the player......Guess What, Boo? You're being played?].

Although, there were few whom tried to hide their relationships, others were quite evident, because they didn't try to hide it, and neither did they care. Besides, this behavior of infidelity has been ongoing for centuries, within our military and it isn't knew. The only difference in then and now is that.....new tricks are learned and new lies are told. Thus, what's so sad is that many spouses stateside and abroad are clearly aware that their spouses are being untrue; some just don't care either, as long if they have piece of a "mane" in a uniform. Consequently, it's sad to observe the vow that was once made before God and family to be made a mockery before God.

What's Matrimony? Is it even worth the ink on the paper, anymore? Just like Ministers. All of a sudden, Ministers are popping up like wild flowers...........everybody wants to be a Minister now. All of a sudden, everybody has a calling......from Athletes, to Sports Commentators, to Rappers, to Gangsters..........Are you serious?

Anyway, I digressed a bit... As a result, I voiced my concern through the military Stars and Stripes. My article posted, on Wednesday February 2, 2005, on page 14. However, when word returned to my base camp of my posted article, addressing infidelity while at war, later many of my other articles addressing racism and other controversial issues never reached the paper to be posted. In other words, my articles had been Bamboozo'd. I soon realized, as long as if wrong is being done, it is alright. But, as soon as right is being done, it's wrong, then you go figure.

Female Shower Trailer

General Soldier Shower Trailers and Porter Potties

Distance won't excuse infidelity

I have been in country for almost a year and my heart goes out to many wives and husbands who remain at home while their spouses are here, not knowing that the vow they took before God, family and friends is worth no more than a candy wrapper thrown on the ground.

Questions: Does distance justify infidelity? Could there have been issues unresolved at home prior to being deployed? If so, would that be enough to justify treading on the hearts of those whom you say you love? How can you say you love your wife, husband or fiancée when you allow yourself to become sexually involved with someone else? Why marry, or even get engaged, when you have such difficulty staying true to your mate, especially during these times of separation? Have you both tried relationship or marital counseling? Or have either one of you sought help from your spiritual adviser, your supreme being? If you have, and nothing seems to work, then do what's right and fair for both of you.

I once read that we as adults "should live so that when your children think of fairness, caring, and integrity, they think of you." Therefore, choose your life's mate carefully; from this one decision will come 90 percent of all your happiness or misery.

In closing, to my male soldiers, if you have at home a good, prime, juicy steak cooked to your perfection; don't throw it away in Iraq on chicken niplets.

And for my female soldiers, if you have a filet mignon at home, please, please, please don't throw it away in Iraq on corndogs.

Sgt. Yolanda Jones
Camp Taji, Iraq

CHAPTER 16

&
Lost Faith; Hopelessness; Feeling Alone and Missing Children
&
Wanted Out
&
Blood Was All I Saw; God's Angel through My Battle Buddy
&
Serenity at Babylon; Combat Relief - A Letter to my Son

For about six month into this war, I was subjected to pure humiliation, was ostracized, berated and provoked by First Sergeant, SFC, the Commander and many of the Commander's Co-Commanders in S-1. They were the "Untouchables." They were my ongoing nightmare and their angle was to break me. I remember the Commander had summons me to report to his office (tent) . At first, I had no idea his reason for summons me. There stood a tent full of Senior Officers, the First Sergeant, the Commander, and I believe two senior NCOs. A tent full of all Caucasian men and, here I stood, one African American Woman. You mean to tell me, it took six to seven of them to come up against to break me down; just because, I had the courage enough to be the voice for those who didn't know how to use their voice.

I felt like I'd committed a crime and I was in a room being interrogated by a bunch of police officers and detectives. However, the problem was that I didn't commit a crime, and they weren't police officers or detectives. Their interrogation went on, for what seemed like eternity. Yet, not once did I shed a tear, and not once did I shake or even appeared nervous. But you can bet, I was damn angry on the inside. Yes, I was boiling like a lid on a tea pot. I wanted it over, and I wanted out. Day in and day out I really felt alone, because I was alone. Soldiers were now being threatened by the First Sergeant not to have any association with me, or they would risk a chance of being demoted for not following a direct order. Once again, the misuse of rank and power was being carefully observed.

I began to question God. What did I do in my past to make me deserve this? What was I about to do in my future that I was being punished in advance for? Why are you not answering my prayers? My questioning God, resulted in me losing my faith in God and the foundation for which I was taught, growing up in church and attending Sunday School; as well as being a step kid to a Minister.... Wow, now that's as deep as it's going to get..........

I then began questioning, if there was ever, a God? My anger and my feeling of hopelessness for myself wouldn't allow me to see the light at the end of the tunnel. If there was a light, it was dim, very dim...........

Well, more and more I became numb. I didn't care anymore. I didn't care if I lived or died. I was ready for whatever happened to me. For, I knew it could be no worse than what I was already experiencing. This was hell right here on earth. The modern day hell. This was my judgment. I was already judged and executed. I knew I had lost me and I didn't know how to get back me.

As I walked, I felt as though I was having an outer body experience, as though my mind was disconnecting from my body. I saw me, but I didn't know who me was. I had missed my children so much that somehow, with all this disconnect I was able to come to peace that, whatever happened to me; while in Iraq, my children will understand and they will be safe with their grandparents. Yes, I had given up. I had no more in me to fight. Therefore, one morning I reported to work, as always; working in the same discomforting, sexist and racist environment. I said nothing to anyone and slowly I was disconnecting more and more. My effect was very flat. You would have had a better chance talking to a stick than with me. As I remembered, I would frequently gaze off as if I was trying to put myself in another place. Any place, but where I was. I believe it was about 0930-10 when I left my work area.

All I saw was blood and dead soldiers lying all around me. It was my vision of what my mind was wanting me to see. I stopped at my tent and made sure that I had all my magazines, and 240 rounds to my weapon. I believe I even had a magazine already in position and my latch was on automatic. Then I head toward the Commander and the First Sergeant and the S-1 work tent. I didn't know why, but I cut through and took a shorter route and I happened to bump into my battle buddy (SSG). As I piece everything together, I remembered my battle buddy telling me that I was scaring him, because I had "that look" in my eyes. I didn't respond, instead I remember crying and telling him that I couldn't take it anymore. That's when my battle buddy told me of his conversation that he and my stepfather shared, back at Fort Hood.

My battle buddy attests that my stepfather had asked him to take care and protect me, and to bring me home safely. So, according to my battle buddy, that was a promise that he was willing to keep. Therefore, he instructed that I stop in and speak with the therapist, of who were only a few tents down, which he watched as I did.

When I walked into the tent, I requested to speak to "someone". I didn't care who, but I knew I needed to talk to someone. I knew I no longer could trust my thoughts, let alone my actions. Immediately, they too saw the look that my battle buddy saw, so, they took possession of my weapon as a result I was then placed on the emergency roster, to be flown to the 785th Combat Relief, in Babylon. Initially, when soldiers are sent to the 785th Combat Relief, it was usually for two to three days stay. However, due to the severity surrounding my circumstances, I remained for seven days. While at Combat Relief, I was placed on a regiment diet, relaxation, counseling, anger-stress management, sleep and daily exercise, and various debriefing / mental health classes.

Since the days-weeks-months that lead up to my break down, I'd begun to experience depressive symptoms clusters; that of decreased appetite, lost of weight, loss of energy/interest in daily activity, slow thinking, difficulty making decisions, difficulty concentrating, sadness, daily irritability and agitation, feeling very guilty, worthless, hopeless, daily preoccupied and consumed with homicidal thoughts as well as insomnia. I was headed down hill very slowly. Combat Relief was what I needed. It had been located in a serenity-like environment. The environment was very calming; the quality of beauty with green grass, trees and a lake. It was nothing like where I was flown in from, which was sand, debris and day to day sounds from RPGS/Mortars.

No, this place was very secluded and very peaceful; momentarily peaceful. For the first few days I had my own room and the mental health staff was awesome. For once I didn't feel judged and neither, was I berated in anyway. The first three to four nights was a cleansing process for me. I cried and cried, and cried some more. I especially cried when one of my assignments was to write a letter to my son, expressing how I felt, since many of my emails and phone calls had gone unanswered. The purpose of the letter was for closure. Closure in that my son needed to know that although, I wasn't angry with him, he's now a young man and that I'm no longer responsible for him. Also, neither will I continue to feel guilty for leaving him and his sister for doing what I signed on the dotted line to do. By the time I wrote that letter, I believe it was at least twenty pages of the long ten inch yellow ruler pad paper. Yes, apparently I had a lot to say, of which much of it had been internalized. Combat Relief was a Great Experience! I felt as though my battery had been recharged.

Outside View of the Ishtar Gate at Babylon

Combat Relief; Serenity Lake

Inside View of One of Sudam's Palace Room Ceiling's)

Inside View of Sudam's Master BedRoom

Outside View of Sudam Palace

CHAPTER 17

Still Being Tried and Tested
&
Returned to Taji; Escaping Death
&
Struggled with the Decision to Go Home for R&R; Not Trusting Myself

After my time spent at Combat Relief was complete, I returned to duty. Although some things had changed for the best, it was proven that some things and people will never change. By this time, word had spread like wild flowers about what had spiraled me to a breaking point. However, my mental state was still being tried and tested, by one individual who's angle was to see me fail. No, it was no longer the Unit or the Commander of the First Sergeant. No, not at all…..instead, it was the racist NCO who, because I didn't give him the time or the day, he was still after me. However, his advances and verbal attacks didn't last long. Ironically, I was now being protected by the same soldiers in my Unit who, in the beginning didn't believe me when I reported about the sexual abuse against our SFC and another female SSG. Apparently, while I was gone the internal investigation continued and for once, the truth was revealed and the SFC was removed. Where? I'll never know. Nevertheless, what I do know was that he was removed away from working with our Unit. More importantly, he was ordered not to come in contact with the SSG, for the remaining of this deployment. That was a great thing………..

Anyway, with regards to this other racist NCO that I returned to work with, let's just say, I now had protection from the male soldiers from my Unit. I never was left alone to work in the connexes and neither did it last long because we were now relocating. And again, we had no knowledge as to where we were going, until we arrived. Hence, we finally arrived and what looked familiar was exactly that. A very familiar place, yes we had returned to Taji; but, this time, the attacks on Taji had increased to a level of higher alert and danger.

There was never a day or an hour that we were not hit. I remember one particular morning, as I was the last female leaving our sleep tent and as I headed out walking down the road towards the job site. ....It wasn't long, for it may have been less than five minutes when I heard a loud noise, behind me. The noise was loud enough and the impact was hard enough to knock me from my feet. I turned around and I noticed smoke coming from the sleep quarters. Yes, it was the same areas where I'd recently just left, maybe had walked a good 250meters, if that.

At this point, I wasn't certain what was the damaged, or even if anyone was injured. Immediately, I ran back to my tent to see if there were any casualties; however, no one was in the tents. Thus, the smoke had come from the shrapnel that had landed on another tent.

Also we noticed the rocket had left a large hole in the cement wall that sat twenty-five paces behind our sleep tents. Wow, the first thing that came to my mind was, "what if." What if, I was standing against the wall, or walking by or even eating breakfast by that wall, like many of us had seldom been doing each morning?

Furthermore, there were many times while my section worked in the motor pool and connexes; we had to continuously run to take cover, due to ongoing explosions and/or attacks from incoming rockets. After a while, I began to wonder with everything that had transpired, resulting in me being flown to Babylon for Combat Relief, was it to prepare my mind to experience a real attack? I began to wonder. Apparently, I'd continued to escape death, time after time after time. I continued to have Angels protecting me, even when I still didn't care if I lived or died.

Well, although I wasn't able to be present to watch my son walk across the stage to obtain his high school diploma, meanwhile, the time had arrived and I was continuously being instructed to take R&R. And, each time I'd declined. I couldn't trust myself to return to Iraq, after being given the opportunity of freedom. The freedom to be away from bondage, this place, that's what it still felt like. I knew that ninety percent of my mind wanted to hide. Go AWOL to another country. I had the availability of funds to go anywhere in the world. However, I knew had I AWOL'd that I would have become a fugitive for life and my children would have become a target for ongoing observation and tapping of their phone conversations to me, as well as my entire family. In the long run, it would had caused a disgrace to my family, let alone an embarrassment to my children.

Likewise, I was no longer feeling numb, I knew I was feeling something which I couldn't explain what.................I had the ability to see clearer and was able to rationalize the pros and cons, as well as the damage that my behavior would do to my children. But what was I really feeling? Why was I afraid to trust myself to do the right thing?

Safety Cover

RoadSide Explosion

Connexes Work Areas

Last Sleep Area & Misssion Location; before leaving Country

CHAPTER 18

The Decision Made to Go Home; Not the Same Person
&
The Decision to Return and Report for Duty; Last Minute Decision (AWOL)
&
Three Months Remaining and Counting

I decided to accept R&R. I had now been in theatre about nine months. I was ready to go; but, not ready to trust myself to return to Iraq. I began having talks to myself, that whatever happens, happens. Thus I began giving away gifts to some of the soldiers whom I respected, and were supportive during my ordeal, in Iraq. Thereafter, I said my good-byes. I remember, there was one female soldier, she was so hilarious. She, along with some other soldiers gave me the name "Mike Jones." She looked at me and told me, "Mike Jones, if you don't come back, I'm going to find you and kick your [blank]." I just smiled and said good-bye. However, when I stepped off the plane my family was all present. But I wasn't joyful, although I remembered exchanging hugs and a smirk.

Neither could I laugh or smile, because I had been through hell and I knew I couldn't share my experience with my family, for I knew they would not understand and neither did I want to break their happy spirit of them seeing and having me home. Nevertheless, I can't recall if I did much with my family. I don't recall if I even saw my son during my visit. I believe my son was enrolled in college and living in another county. Awkwardly feeling, I remembered speaking briefly to my uncle and telling him that I needed to reserve a room for the two weeks that I was going to be home at one of the hotels that he was employed with. Therefore, he accommodated me. I knew I didn't want to be around my family the entire two weeks. I didn't want to hear noise, yelling (family talking loud), and watching television loud.

My family had a tendency to watch television so loud that you could hear it from outside. I wanted peace and quiet. For the first week home, I spent time alone in my hotel. I didn't want to entertain anyone, not even my own children. I needed solitude. Even when I decided to spend the second and last week with my daughter, it didn't feel the same prior to me getting deployed. Something had changed............I had changed. I wondered if my daughter noticed a change in me. The night before I was to return to Iraq, I decided not to allow my daughter to spend the night with me. Therefore, I gave her a hug and a kiss. I told her that I loved her and for her to relay a message to her brother that I will always love him. I then took her home to her grandparent's.

Again, I needed to know what my mind was going to do. What was my mind plans? I still didn't trust my mind. But I knew I was not the same person, who received deployment orders on November 22, 2003.

Honestly, I no longer knew who I was, but I knew what I had become. Disconnected.

The morning came and I laid in the bed until it was time to check out the hotel. I was still confused. I took one of my antidepressant pills, drank a cup of coffee and I checked out the hotel. As I played back the events of this morning, the morning seemed so dismal, as though I was preparing to go to a funeral. It felt very dark within. My heart was racing, palms were sweaty, I had a pit in my stomach, for I felt nauseated and very light headed and my body was going through some physiological changes.

As I arrived to the airport, and made my presence known, I sat and I watched the line of soldiers check in. I was now ready to make a detour and pay for another ticket to board a flight elsewhere. However, as I was about to get up, I heard a familiar male's voice. He was a soldier and a very loyal friend of whom I had joined on multiples convoys and whom was very much aware of the hell that I had sustained. He approached me and said in a very calm and non-judgmental tone, "It's good to see you, Sgt. Jones, I don't care what you were planning to do, or what you were about to do, I'm glad you're here." Although I was able to hold back my tears, I responded with a smile and said, "Thank You." All of a sudden and out of nowhere, the energy I felt off of his words of encouragement was all I needed, as a extra push to give me the strength to finish it out. I now had three months remaining, and I was prepared and ready to stick it out.

After all, I have already weathered the jest of the Hell. What's three more months? Well, because of the discomforting events that occurred, there were already reports that I wasn't returning, and that I may AWOL. Even though the flight was very long, for once I felt that my voice was heard, in advocating for the rights of others. Soldiers were happy to see me which was evident by their many smiles, laughers and greetings. I even recall one male soldier shouting out to me, "You can't keep a strong black woman down." I just laughed. All of a sudden, I began to receive a sense of respect from the same soldiers whom initially turned their backs, and didn't support me or my cause. Although I was receiving all this recognition, my guards remained up. **I trusted no one.**

Even the First Sergeant, Commander and all of the Co-Commanders were acknowledging my presence. Wow, what a flip of a coin. I even recall receiving an official apology from the Major and the Colonel. Many of my male counterparts in my section began apologizing for not being receptive, and not believing the truths against their favorite SFC whom they've always looked up to and admired.

Just to think, had I AWOL'd, I would've never experienced this amazing turn around. And to know that I was part of revealing something that even today, to often it remains unrecorded or ignored in today's society. Especially, with regards to racism, sexual assaults, sexual harassments and domestic violence in the schools system, work places (especially in private agencies, who set their own agency rules and usually get away with abusing their employees). Also, many of our police departments, City/State Counsel Boards and Elected Officials are not exempt.

CHAPTER 19

Count Down to Home
&
Awards Distributed and Ceremonies
&
He's Back!
&
Leaving Theatre; Deployment Ends
&
What Was the Purpose of the Mission? Did I Miss Something?

I began to count down the number of days remaining for me to return home. I was now excited and very happy to return. However, toward the latter of our time in Iraq, there were ceremonies and awards distributed. On the other hand, I didn't care to receive an award. As a result, I trashed and threw away or gave away many of my awards to another female soldier. You ask me why? Because, these awards meant nothing to me; especially, when he (SFC) had returned. Yes, during our ceremonies, he returned. Although he stood in the back, he still shouldn't have been allowed to participate in the award ceremony. He was a disgrace to the uniform, and he'd lost all respect from his soldiers.

Why was he back?

Was it to prove that as long if you've tenure, or is approaching retirement that you're untouchable? Yes, that was exactly the message that I received. So now, what was to come of this female soldier (SSG) when she returns to the states? Is he going to beg for her forgiveness? Also, like the majority of domestic violence victims, who allow their abusers to return and start over with the honey moon phase? This is pure disgust, and you ask why I didn't want to accept any awards?.............

For what?

One good thing that came out of this was, even though he returned, he wasn't allowed to come around me, let alone inches near me. A matter of fact, he really had very little contact if any, with his platoon or even the female soldier. That was good. Besides, who would have listened to him anyway? He'd lost all of our respect. He was no longer in charge of our platoon. Now, it was time to leave theatre, for the deployment had finally come to an end. Therefore, we began loading up and clearing out, and heading to the wash point to wash our vehicles, before loading them onto the cargos for travel.

I then began to wonder.

What was the purpose for this mission? I never knew.

Besides, the majority of the time spent in country was moving from one location to the next. Our section simply worked on vehicles, managed the vehicle parts and inventory, as well as transferred parts to various shops for repair. Other sections of the Unit were the engineering components, which they build throughout the deployment. Then, of course there were many in my section and throughout the unit who participated in raids outside of Taji with other Units that resulted in many of our soldiers being injured, as well as other causalities from various Units. So, what was the purpose of this mission? What did I miss? I don't ever recall being told the initial reason for the mission, even at the start of the deployment. Were we initially supposed to catch Sudam? Or were we suppose to finish the 507th mission, whatever that was? Or were we there to rebuild Iraq? Or were we there to catch Osama Bin Laden? What? Or were we there as retaliation from what happen on 9/11? Or did we get caught up in some unfinished business that was passed down from our political leaders. What?

Many soldiers from our Unit will forever be scarred mentally and physically and many soldiers were killed from other Units, during my entire deployment in Iraq. Question? Was this Necessary?

CHAPTER 20

Scarred, But Not Broken; Angels Come in All Race, Ethnicity, Professional and Social Economic Status

It took me six years to write this book, due to the materials that were initially going to be included. However, I knew if I'd written this book upon my return from deployment, it wouldn't have had a purpose, but would have been written out of anger. Besides, after years of soul searching, allowing myself time to heal, as well as receiving legal advice, I was now ready to tell my story. Even though my healing is a daily and ongoing recovery process, I frequently have nightmares and flashbacks which are easily triggered by certain smells, sounds and obnoxious people, who remind me so much of the poor leadership; in which, I was subjected to. Or, even those people whom I come in contact with on a daily basis whom, many tends to take life for granted or abuse the system or even their authority.

It becomes more challenging when I have to work under management who appear to be concern for their own welfare and professional growth; opposed to the welfare and professional or personal growth of the staff. This alone, is definitely and has been a major trigger for me. Hence, during my ordeal, I learned that good people come in all race, ethnicity, professional and social economic status. It's just the rotten few that tend to get through without a spot or wrinkle; which takes individuals and soldiers like me to take on the challenge of seeing justice prevailing. And, don't think I hadn't thought about some of the negative responses that this book may receive, after its release. I've no doubt, my book will be seen by many as very controversial....However, I say to anyone who has been offended by what was said.......

As a result, if whatever I said caused any discomfort that may have igniting a positive change in our **Military** or in our **Social System**, so be it.....then, I have been successful in my intent of advocating for the truth. Too often, people in general, want to sit back and complain about what is not being done. Yet, those same people never seem to have a solution. And, if they do, they'll sit on it and wait until someone else takes the initiative, to eradicate for change. Then, once positive change has been made, those same people will push themselves to the forefront to say, "You know, that's exactly what I was thinking about." Yeah, ...O....K and my name is "Little Red Riding Hood".........
Whatever! Well, I'm not one of those who sit on the back and complain..............I make it happen, and I don't have to compromise my integrity in doing so.

Although, I experienced the good, the bad, and certainly the ugly, there were some good A-Co 980th male and female soldiers who made the latter of my experience worth living. It was these soldiers; my Angels, who allowed me to see my purpose for experiencing all what I did and to be that voice for millions of victims, dead and alive; whom were and have been victimized for so long; but, never had the strength to endure the fight................ I Thank You!

And, although it may seem to some that I didn't take my experience seriously, due to many of the jokes, or even the smart comments, or rebuttals that I may have made......Well, believe it or not, those smart rebuttals or comments is **MY THERAPY**....
It's what gets me through **one more day**. Because, sometimes I don't even have the strength to even want to get up out the bed, just because of the triggers and the obnoxious people I have to interact with on a day to day basis, whether in the supermarket or driving on the highway, or even at work...............I always believe

that someone may say something, or may do something that will remind me of the poor leadership that placed me in a living hell. Moreover, it may remind me, as well as being under the direction of an abusive SFC who was a womanizer. So, yes some days are better than others...............Nevertheless, this is **MY THERAPY!**

Furthermore, to add insult to injury, I had been subjected to the racism of those in leadership, who were the **"untouchables."** Nevertheless, they were able to get away with whatever they wanted, and did whatever they wanted to do, and with whomever they wanted to do it to. So, don't get it twisted..................I took my experience very seriously...............We all just have our own ways of handling things. Yes, I can continue to go on for another six years and let this experience eat away at my inner core or I can continue to do exactly what I'm doing, by writing and speaking about the truth, as well as advocating for victims, whom don't as of **yet** have the strength to voice for themselves.

So, although I've walked away from this experience and have been **scarred** mentally and physically, and although transitioning has been difficult for me, and although I struggle day to day to manage my PTSD, I've a stronger relationship with both of my adult children, now than ever before. More importantly, **I'm Scarred, but not broken........**

Yolanda Jones is a Native New Yorker Disabled Iraqi Veteran and a Survivor of Domestic Violence. Ms. Jones currently holds an Associate's and a Bachelor's Degree in Criminal Justice and a Master's Degree in Counseling and Development, upon which she obtained from Texas Woman's University. Ms. Jones future goal is to become a Motivational and Public Speaker, in advocating for Victims of Domestic Violence and Racial Discrimination; Nationally and Internationally. Ms. Jones ultimate goal is to do <u>Whatever is in God's Plan</u>...............

CPSIA information can be obtained
at www.ICGtesting.com
Printed in the USA
FSOW01n1954230215
5376FS